"What a chance!" cries Hyena.
"To dance will be cool."

Hyena ballerina

Russell Punter

Illustrated by David Semple

Ten students are wanted
at Swan's Ballet School.

...in my frilly silk tutu
and pink satin shoes."

Swan brings them together.

"Let's see what you've got."

Hyena springs forward
and spins on the spot.

She stands high
on tiptoe,

leans back
on a chair,

twirls lightly
in circles,

and floats
through the air.

"I can prance
like a princess...

...or glide
like a fairy."

Swan soon loses interest.

"Too spotty and hairy!"

Hyena feels weepy.

She sticks out her chin.

"What luck!" shouts out Duck.
"You're just what I need!

You must join my stage show. You're bound to succeed."

"My acts can jump hurdles,
or balance a ball,

STAGE DOOR

but ballet like that will
attract one and all."

"Not a bit, don't you worry.
You'll fit in just fine."

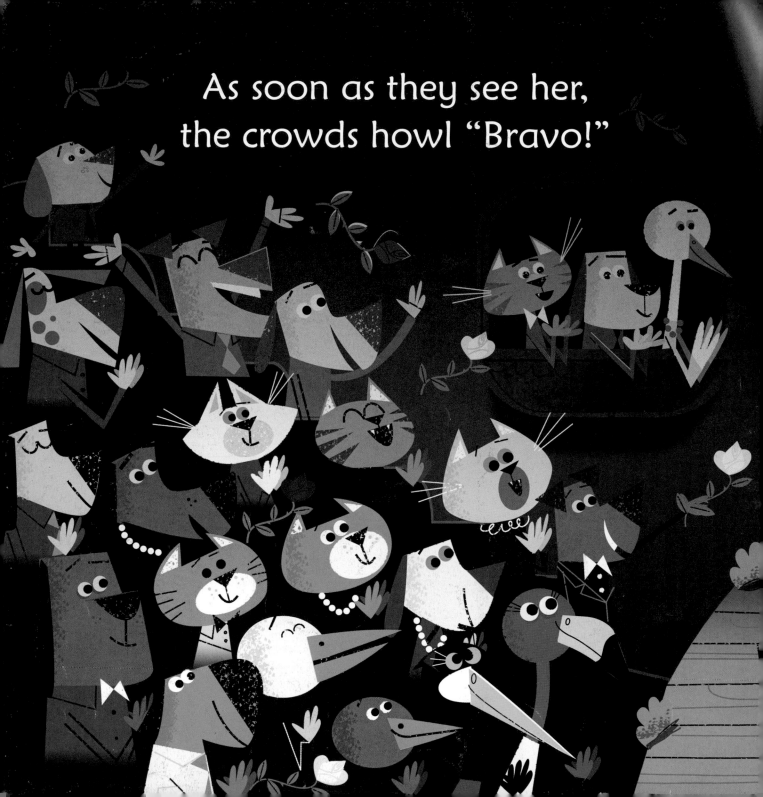

As soon as they see her,
the crowds howl "Bravo!"

Hyena Ballerina is the star of the show.

About phonics

Phonics is a method of teaching reading used extensively in today's schools. At its heart is an emphasis on identifying the *sounds* of letters, or combinations of letters, that are then put together to make words. These sounds are known as phonemes.

Starting to read
Learning to read is an important milestone for any child. The process can begin well before children start to learn letters and put them together to read words. The sooner children can discover books and enjoy stories and language, the better they will be prepared for reading themselves, first with the help of an adult and then independently.

You can find out more about phonics on the Usborne Very First Reading website, **www.usborne.com/veryfirstreading** (US readers go to **www.veryfirstreading.com**). Click on the **Parents** tab at the top of the page, then scroll down and click on **About synthetic phonics**.

Phonemic awareness

An important early stage in pre-reading and early reading is developing phonemic awareness: that is, listening out for the sounds within words. Rhymes, rhyming stories and alliteration are excellent ways of encouraging phonemic awareness.

In this story, your child will soon identify the *ee* sound, as in **hyena** and **ballerina**. Look out, too, for rhymes such as **prove** – **move** and **chance** – **dance**.

Hearing your child read

If your child is reading a story to you, don't rush to correct mistakes, but be ready to prompt or guide if he or she is struggling. Above all, do give plenty of praise and encouragement.

Edited by Jenny Tyler and Lesley Sims
Designed by Sam Whibley and Hope Reynolds

Reading consultants: Alison Kelly and Anne Washtell

First published in 2017 by Usborne Publishing Ltd., Usborne House, 83-85 Saffron Hill, London EC1N 8RT, England.
www.usborne.com Copyright © 2017 Usborne Publishing Ltd.